The Captivating Power of Storytelling

Pervasiveness of storytelling in our daily lives

By

Lisa A. Kim

Table of content

Introduction

Every element of our life, including politics, the arts, and economics, are impacted by storytelling. How might narrative help us fight apathy?

Storytelling has long been one of the most powerful methods for people to connect. We develop empathy, establish trust, and cement stronger connections as we listen to one other's stories. Additionally, it is a powerful method for fusing meaning and aim with emotions.

Children who participate in storytelling experience a variety of psychological and educational benefits, including greater vocabulary, improved communication skills, and an enhanced ability to visualize spoken words. It is unclear, nevertheless, how storytelling affects children's brains in this way.

Storytelling has long been one of the most effective ways for people to connect. Sharing our experiences fosters empathy, establishes trust, and strengthens bonds between people. It is also a very powerful approach to connecting feelings with purpose and meaning. A story activates parts of the brain in the listener that enable them to embody the story and their ideas. This is called neural coupling, in which the brain's activities sync up and release the feel-good hormone called dopamine.

The art of storytelling involves narrating a tale in a captivating, compelling, or dramatic manner.

Without utilizing a book, telling stories involves standing or sitting while narrating the story using one's voice or sign language.

Everyone tells stories.

We all naturally tell stories and do so in one way or another every day while interacting with others, gossiping or sharing secrets, or recalling an event that was dramatic, thrilling, or horrific.

Sometimes we do it in a funny, dramatic, or stunning way.

Chapter one

How Can Children Benefit from Storytelling?

Children have a lot of inquiries and imaginations in their early years. As they become older, kids get more curious and want to know everything about the things they see every day.

Think back to your early years when you enjoyed spending all day listening to your grandparents tell tales. Miss those times, am I right?

Now consider your child. Is he experiencing those moments? Those captivating tales that pique his desire to learn more and stories that spark wild imaginations Interesting stories, dramatic dialogue, oddball characters, and fantastical circumstances! Unusual language and astounding sound effects must captivate and engage the child. All of which will improve your children's ability to memorize information and pay attention.

Storytelling is important since it is the most fascinating and captivating activity you can do to develop your child's personality. You can simply share your own real-life experiences, frame a new story, or read out a good story from a book. Kids cherish stories. Stories have the power to transform ordinary events into extraordinary ones by imagining new realities, feelings, and concepts. They can guide us on wonderful excursions and teach us empathy. They are capable of making us smile, sob, or jump in alarm before consoling us with a pleasant conclusion. We learn how to enjoy a narrative from a very young age, both for pure enjoyment and to aid in our quest for self- and world-understanding.

Importance of storytelling for children

Kids love to read stories! Children are greatly captivated by the amazing illustrations in the books, which depict ideas, locations, and creatures. In addition to being enjoyable, storytelling has a plethora of advantages that promote early childhood development. Let's now examine the 10 advantages of storytelling and their effects on kids.

1. **Recognize their origins and cultures:** The early childhood learning program includes stories heavily. Your young ones will learn about and feel a connection to the various traditions and roots present in the family if you share historical and traditional tales with them. Share interesting events, occasions,

and historical occurrences. Your children will learn about the many customs around the world. Telltales from all across the world as well. This will foster a feeling of cultural awareness among your children.

2. **Educates children about ethics and virtues:**Storytelling is a favorite pastime for children of all ages. In their everyday lives, they make an effort to imitate the traits of the characters and the circumstances in the stories. In light of this, we can conclude that storytelling can significantly influence a child's traits. So, keep in mind to specify them precisely. Share engrossing

tales as well to help them develop virtues like thankfulness, courage, wisdom, and many others, such as being honest and truthful. Tell them tales that demonstrate the value of morals and ethical ideals in life. Always finish your tales with morals, lessons in ethics, and important messages.

3. **Increases the ability to listen and think**: Children prefer to talk more than they do to listen. And this situation is made more clear when you tell boring, vague stories. They listen to stories with less focus, which weakens their ability to think clearly. Make sure the storytime is

entertaining and active. This will catch their interest, which will result in better comprehension and listening abilities. Therefore, use stories that show pure humor and concise themes to improve their communication skills.

4. **Increases verbal fluency**Stories are a new source for early childhood learning programs nowadays. Reading aloud to children enables them to become familiar with new words, phrases, and languages. Pronunciation and social abilities are routinely improved through this procedure. Furthermore, reading the words and sentences aloud

increases comprehension and hastens learning. Therefore, always try new terms throughout your storytime.

5. **Enhances emotional intelligence and empathy:** Stories aid in increasing awareness while also enhancing emotional intelligence and emotional control. Your youngster can learn to be more considerate of other people's needs and their own by participating in stories. Children unconsciously learn to think for others as they engage in listening and comprehending activities. One becomes a better person as a result

of having this sense of empathy and concern for others. Use this aspect of children's psychology to help them develop their emotional intelligence and become more aware of how their behavior affects others.

6. **Increases self-assurance in speaking**:Hearing clearly defined stories helps people expand their vocabulary, which directly impacts how they speak while talking. And it should go without saying that if they express their words and sentences well, it will inevitably boost their confidence. Make sure to teach new terms to your child

during story time and encourage them to spell them out clearly.

7. **Memory and Concentration Improvement:** By incorporating challenging concepts, storytelling can be used as a clever early childhood learning technique. You may utilize storytelling to improve your kids' attention spans and memory capacity. Read them an amiable story out loud, then ask them to explain the lesson it contains. As an alternative, you pause and ask them to restate the narrative up to this point. Alternatively, you can ask them to provide a quick summary of the

story a day or two later. You will gain a better understanding of your kids' ability to focus and memorize information thanks to this. Use this entertaining learning method to hone vocabulary, boost focus, and fortify memory.

8. **Creative and inventive thinking** Fictional and realistic stories encourage children to use their imaginations and be creative. Narrative tales that depict a variety of civilizations, occasions, fantasies, settings, and characters are not just fantastical. The children's creativity and imagination will be enhanced as a result of this, which will invoke

components of intellectual thinking. For the best chance of producing an imaginative thinker, choose a variety of themes and subjects.

9. **Increases interest in the learning process:** Parents or mentors should be aware of when to pause during storytelling sessions. The correct amount of story pauses pique the child's interest and makes them want to know more. Their curiosity and desire to learn aid in their growth and learning. Use this innovative early childhood learning strategy to inspire your child to

learn more and more by putting it into practice

10. **Promote active engagement in demanding circumstances:** Children frequently become confused as a result of difficult circumstances. Tell tales about various characters that encounter adversity. This idea will undoubtedly prepare students to assess specific answers in challenging future situations.

The Benefits of Storytelling for Children Learning a Second Language

For your child's native language, second language, and any foreign language your family learns, storytelling has a powerful impact on language development. The advantages of storytelling and language development in youngsters have been demonstrated by research throughout the years.

Children with regular exposure to a range of stories demonstrate higher developed oral language skills. The procedure also helps kids expand their vocabulary. They also study sentence structure and syntax.

Storytelling requires attentive listening, which promotes learning. Well-crafted storytelling is humorous, dramatic, and fascinating, so learning seems to flow naturally. When children are engaged in a storytelling session, a movie is playing in their heads.

Many families schedule a child's storytime before bed. During quiet time, some families also read aloud or read to their children. A lot of parents of small children also go for storytime at their local public libraries. However, because of the pandemic, storytime has switched from libraries to online venues. It is unique. However, it provides more options for you and your child. More enjoyment is had,when there is more language. The stories allow you to travel. Additionally, you don't have to board a plane this time. It takes place virtually. The most important thing is to remain consistent wherever your kids attend storytime. The input of listening is the same as input in reading. Both can be provided simultaneously via stories.

Before producing the target language, your youngster needs a lot of high-quality information. That is a comparable approach to learning the first language. Speaking starts after listening,Writing comes after reading.

Your child requires content that is appropriate for their ability level to learn a second or foreign language. You can include easy follow-up activities like coloring, drawing, sequencing, and question and Answer to help children remember the stories and strengthen their literacy skills after each storytime.

Chapter two

Storytelling for Leaders:How Can Leaders Influence, Teach, and Inspire Others?

Rapid change is occurring in the business environment. The reporting hierarchy has become more complicated, and organizational structures are flattered. Worldwide distribution of customers, clients, and employees. Due to information overload, people are having trouble.

Nevertheless, in this ever-changing world, leaders still need to be able to influence and persuade. They have the chance to do this through storytelling. Since telling stories is at the core of any successful organization, a leader needs to be a skilled storyteller. The type of leadership exhibited by the executive team is determined by the tales exchanged at the boardroom table.

To influence employee morale and provide direction, executives must be able to articulate their future goals to their staff.

A leader's job includes motivating, inspiring, and influencing others around them. That includes their personnel, their stakeholders, and the clients of their business. Leaders can make their impact known in a variety of contexts, from informal interactions to "management by walking about," from meetings, presentations to mentoring and coaching, and even inside formal learning programs. But regardless of the method used to give it, impact doesn't merely come from sharing knowledge or quoting statistics from a PowerPoint slide presentation. Leaders have an impact when they communicate with others in ways that facilitate understanding, help people remember, and motivate them to take action. Influence involves both thought and behavior change. It is what enables learning to be enduring.

With the use of stories, leaders can motivate their teams to succeed, ally themselves with investors and communities, and interact with clients more successfully. A leader's success depends on their ability to tell a story that is genuine, reliable, and appealing.

For a very small investment, storytelling may have a significant impact on the organization. It is understandable why companies and executives would want to learn how to make compelling stories.

Good stories have a variety of qualities, including the ability to surprise us, provoke thought, stay with us, and aid with concept retention in a way that text cannot.

The business has never been more eager for stories than it is now, according to Alexander Mackenzie, a storytelling expert from Cranfield University.

Why is storytelling Crucial to Leadership?

The advantage goes unfairly to great storytellers. By articulating a compelling vision, businesses can attract and retain the best employees, interact more effectively with the press and media, raise money for their project or company more simply, and forge commercial connections more swiftly.

Good storytellers make good leaders.

The lesson behind a story is more likely to stick in people's minds when they can relate to it. This holds whether we are speaking informally or in a professional setting, like a presentation

The following are some of the main advantages of storytelling:

Highlight the behaviors you want to see in teams.

makes technical data and knowledge far more memorable

and engages your audience deeply, not just briefly

Let's discuss the wisdom and principles that form your leadership style.

encourages and inspires others to support your cause

encourages others to take action

What characteristics distinguish a superb story?

Persons with a strong presence and effective communication skills are frequently remembered when asked to name the notable people in their lives, whether they were involved in politics, media, or education. These individuals are frequently connected to the tales we can recall about them.

To make a tale memorable, focus on delivering on these three points:

Inform - impart our knowledge intellectually

Engage - to speak in a way that grabs the audience's attention

Inspire: to inspire is to spark one's imagination.

We switch between the three stages automatically when we are communicating effectively. However, in a professional setting, we frequently find ourselves concentrating on the first, providing information to others without engaging or motivating them.

Once the lesson has been learned, you should concentrate on delivery and engagement. Consider how you can use your story to inspire others.

A story can be divided approximately into three parts: the problem, the journey, and the solution:

The problem: What problems did you find in your industry, and why? What service or item was lacking?

The journey: How did you go about looking for a solution to this issue? How did you create your product or service?

The resolution: How will your product or service affect the market or address the issue?

Stories deal with change.

All tales revolve around change, whether that change is imposed upon us (for instance, by a rival) or chosen by us (for example by creating a new product line). At times of transition and decision, our lives turn in one direction or the other. To influence and persuade others of your message, you simply need to identify the significance of these times for your tale.

The most compelling narratives center on errors, failures, and catastrophes

The greatest stories frequently involve challenges that must be overcomed, like rebounding from disappointing product sales or missing a flight due to traffic

What creates suspense and adds passion to your story is the error, failure, or calamity. The challenge needs to serve as both the story's turning point and its most memorable element.

Another excellent source of knowledge is stories about leaders who made mistakes in their careers and what they discovered as a result. People can deal with situations in a risk-free manner because they identify with stories so strongly and imagine how they would have done in similar scenarios. The added benefit for leaders is that by sharing a personal story, they may position themselves as more approachable, express underlying principles, provide insight into the development of their own experience and knowledge, and most likely encourage people who want to learn more.

There are two sorts of Storytelling

There are two types of storytelling: the more common one you might tell a friend and the more strategic one. The most important distinction is that with strategic storytelling, you're attempting to create a vision for the future that hasn't yet occurred. But the common pattern that underlies all narratives is what emotionally connects us to them.

Questions to consider before choosing your story strategy

Since leadership is storytelling and leaders are storytellers, all leaders must be able to tell tales. Building a strategic vision and getting everyone on board takes a lot of time and effort. When choosing your story strategy, take into account the following:

What are the repercussions of victory or defeat? What is the ultimate goal or vision? (For instance, your product might be surpassed by a rival.)

What are the challenges you'll face as you work toward achieving your end goal? (For instance, political barriers or even a lack of funding or staff)

How are you going to get through these challenges?

Can you mention any more successful similar stories, whether they were from a different company or a coworker? This will encourage people.

Chapter three

Storytelling in the business.

What does telling a story mean in business?

When engaging with present or potential consumers, storytelling in business refers to the technique of telling a tale as opposed to listing facts. Giving their clients a narrative to remember them by, helps firms stand out from their rivals. Large brands can engage their audience more deeply and personally with the use of stories in the business world. Business storytelling is a powerful communication strategy that enables brands to engage with customers. Businesses can inform clients about their products or introduce them to their brand by creating a story. It's crucial to develop storytelling skills if you want to connect with your audience. Customers are more likely to choose a brand when it appears more approachable. Customers of all types can be reached through storytelling. It could be utilized to clarify technical information or to show prospects why they ought to pick your brand over another. The aspects that are unimportant to a customer's decision to choose a business are omitted in business storytelling.

A tale comprises specifics such as team motivators, the principles and values of the company, knowledge of the target audience, and a chronological flow of facts and information that guide the audience through the narrative. Through storytelling, companies can demonstrate to customers that they are much more than just a well-known brand. It proves that they are telling a story.

In this chapter, we go through the advantages of sharing stories in business and how to craft the ideal one.

The advantages of storytelling in business

Storytelling in business is a potent marketing strategy. The use of storytelling in business has numerous advantages, including:

Customers are more deeply and personally engaged by stories. Employees may feel more connected to a company and gain a deeper understanding of its principles with their aid.

Make a lasting impression: The longer someone remembers a product or brand, the more probable it is that they will buy it. People are more inclined to remember stories because of their resonance.

Triggering emotions and feelings is important for brands to engage with consumers. Emotions are more likely to drive action.

Increase customer loyalty: People stick with companies that they have a connection to on an emotional level. Stories are more likely to inspire devoted clients since they convey concepts in a manner that customers are accustomed to hearing.

Gives firms a competitive edge: By building a relationship with their audience, businesses can use storytelling to stand out from rivals. They can leave enduring impressions by using stories.

Convince customers to act: Converting customers is the main objective of most marketing initiatives. Customers are moved to action by stories,

The following actions are to be considered while employing storytelling in business.

- **Select a target audience:**The first stage in business storytelling is figuring out to whom you are telling your tale. You should also decide on the story's purpose or objective at this point. Are you attempting to sell something? Do you want to introduce customers to your brand? The person who is most likely to use your brand should be taken into account while trying to sell a product or raise brand recognition. Conducting market research will reveal who your target audience is. Who are your present customers? Which clients are you trying to attract? Before creating your tale, develop a client persona to help you understand your target. Identifying your audience can aid in your decision regarding the publication of your narrative. Will you send it to me as an email? Will you release a multi-platform video?

- **Perfect your message:**Once you've identified your target audience, think about the message you want to convey to them. You might draw attention to a concern shared by many of your clients or choose a moral you want to spread. By determining who you are telling the narrative, what message you want to convey, and what lasting impression you want to make on your readers,can improve your story. You should also think about how you might appeal to the reader's emotions through your message. These specifics will establish the framework for your story.

- **Pick a hero** Every engaging tale has a hero. This is the someone or thing that is put forth to address the issue. Make the hero relatable to the reader, your target audience, by how you present them. Think of this person as the link between your brand's customers and itself. Create them so that they accurately reflect the requirements, wants, and most frequent issues of your clients. The objective is for your target customer to identify with this individual.there is a conflict and a resolution in every story. You are better able to establish a personal connection with your audience by placing your hero in a conflict that is shared by all of your customers.

- **Compose your story**: Once the specifics of your story have been established, it is time to write it. You may write a rough draft and then revise it to make it more understandable. You might also employ a copywriter to write your story in the tone and voice of your company.write the conclusion to the narrative centered on your product or service. Potential clients can then picture how your company's goods or services can benefit them. In this phase, a call-to-action is also created. After reading your story, what precise action do you want your audience to take? Business storytelling has the potential to persuade more customers to act.

Tips for enhancing your business storytelling

Ensure simplicity: Making your story longer than necessary or including too many details can turn off your audience.

Get comfortable telling stories: You will get better at telling your narrative to others as you use it more often.

Be truthful: Honesty and sincerity will improve your audience engagement with your story and brand.

Add worth: Pick elements or passages from the story that will best enrich the lives of your audience.

Make it enjoyable: The audience's attention can be held for a longer period in entertaining stories.

Make it inclusive: Universal stories can appeal to a wider range of readers.

Chapter Four

Using stories as a teaching tool

One of the oldest methods of instruction is storytelling. It's something that everyone does and has done for as long as anyone can remember. We tell stories to connect and bond with one another. Teachers are storytellers. Consider all the occasions when you have needed to relate a concept or aid students in understanding a subject. You may not even be aware of it, but you already employ the teaching approach of storytelling, which has been passed down via culture. The earliest method of communication is through oral storytelling, but there are also written visual, and digital forms.

Why is Storytelling a Successful Teaching Technique?

Storytelling is a strategy that, according to research, aids children in understanding their surroundings. Additionally, it aids children in imagining themselves in the storyteller's conditions. The capacity to recount events chronologically is a fundamental academic skill that all pupils must possess. A child's reading development is greatly aided by reading and listening to stories. Stories assist students in better absorbing relevant information while also making studying more enjoyable.

Storytelling in the Classroom: How to Use It

There are several ways to incorporate Storytelling in the classroom. Here are some approaches.

To Begin a New Topic

A wonderful technique to introduce a new topic is by telling a story. Acknowledge it as an icebreaker,Even before you teach a subject, it can help pupils relate to it and get interested in it. By relating a tale concerning the brand-new subject you're about to cover, you can activate prior knowledge. Engaging kids in reader's theater is another strategy for utilizing storytelling to introduce a new subject. Simply pick the subject and create a script that the students can perform. A narrative about a bear getting ready to hibernate and discovering all of his companions in the cave may be a good way to introduce the new topic of hibernating mammals.

To Draw the interest of Unmotivated Learners

As long as you uniquely tell stories, like by incorporating them into a game or enjoyable activity, storytelling can help encourage your uninterested students.

To Present a Concept

Not everyone finds it simple to retain hard facts. This is when good storytelling can save the day. Digital storytelling can be an efficient approach to explaining a challenging idea in today's age of videos, iPads, and podcasts. Students may learn and remember the material more creatively and vividly by using digital storytelling with videos, graphics, applications, and music.

Stories can also be communicated via images and illustrations, thus digital storytelling isn't the only technique to explain a challenging idea. Ask pupils to write a narrative using a series of images or visuals that represent a certain theme.

To Improve a Subject

A dry subject can become interesting when taught through storytelling. It can make it more engaging and even inspire kids to want to learn more about the subject. Many kids find it difficult to learn Math, but via storytelling, they can create their word problems to help them understand it. Storytelling is a potent tool for making any lesson into an adventure.

I believe that Storytelling is more than just narrating a story; it also evokes our emotions. It can bring us to tears or laughter, and it fosters connections with others and memory of past events. Overall, it's an effective means of communication that can enable anyone to relate to or perceive the world from another's perspective.

Students who have enjoyed listening to stories in class frequently beg for more stories, and they also feel inspired and encouraged to make up their own stories to tell, act out, or illustrate in other ways. The act of storytelling appeals to a variety of learning styles and personalities, allowing everyone—from the most reserved to the most outgoing students—to engage in a way that they find enjoyable. This can be anything from silent listening to acting.

Chapter Five

Advertisement and marketing

People want to connect with brands and businesses, and the best advertisements achieve this by being relatable or evoking emotions. Storytelling can be a powerful marketing strategy to improves the effectiveness and engagement of employees

A firm only succeeds when its people do, as they are the lifeblood of the enterprise and its greatest asset.

Using storytelling, you may create the right culture at work. This goes beyond simply articulating a compelling vision; rather, tells stories about the company's development, challenges, core principles, and goals. Tell your staff what's essential and let them know what it means for them. They will have something to believe in as a result, which will enhance their motivation to work and their belief in the business. Making your employees a part of the bigger picture of the business is simply giving them a higher feeling of purpose and significance. Encourage your staff to share their own experiences to advance this.

In summary

Storytelling has a much greater ability to persuade people than citing statistics. You may use stories to connect with any audience and motivate them to take action. In fact, since telling tales is such a potent instrument, it is your duty as a storyteller to use them to make your community's life better. Nearly all human inventions predate the art of storytelling. It also comes as no surprise given the incredible ability of stories to completely captivate our attention, arouse our emotions, and envelop us in intriguing and bizarre worlds.

But stories are more than simply enjoyable distractions or thrilling experiences—they're also useful tools. In reality, one of the earliest and most effective ways to spread important knowledge and influence behavior is through storytelling. And that still holds now just as it did in the early history of humans.

Today, it can be challenging to identify a successful brand that does not have a compelling backstory. Stories give context, meaning, and a feeling of direction. The majority of people are more responsive to tales than to facts or data because stories make it easier for us to relate, empathize, and remember. Because of this, more and more companies are realizing the value of narrative.

www.ingramcontent.com/pod-product-compliance
Lightning Source LLC
Chambersburg PA
CBHW060942130726
48001CB00003B/1029